Atget,
Life in Paris

Guillaume Le Gall

Atget, Life in Paris

Translated from the French
by Brian Holmes

POCKET *✶* ARCHIVES

HAZAN

Cover: Ragpicker, avenue des Gobelins. June 1901

© Éditions Hazan, Paris, 1998
Editor: Éric Reinhardt
Design: Atalante
Production: Maya Masson
Color separation: Seleoffset, Torino
Printing: Milanostampa, Farigliano

ISBN: 2 85025 641 2
ISSN : 1275-5923
Printed and Bound in Italy

Contents

Atget and Urban Theater
7

Petits Métiers
49

Old Shops and Signs
107

Vitrines
183

Atget and
Urban Theater

From the surrealists, who published a number of his prints, to the work of Walker Evans and Lee Friedlander, which betrays the evident influence of his art, Eugène Atget (1857-1927) has incontestably become one of the cardinal references in the history of photography.[1] Peter Gallassi, the director of the photography department at the Museum of Modern Art in New York, recently confirmed the photographer's importance when he stated that in his eyes, Atget was "one of the great artists of the twentieth century."[2] Others have not always been of the same opinion, preferring to point to the occasional weaknesses in his vast production, doubting Atget's mastery over both his art and his choice of subjects, encouraging the legend of a naive and ill-informed photographer. But need one stress the hastiness of the polemical judgment that so often accompanies the reception of Atget's production, a judgment that refuses it the status of a veritable *oeuvre?*[3] Wouldn't it be more just to consider Atget as an author of documents imbued with political concerns,

subtle enough that we can still look at them and learn
from them today?

Atget's work is structured by a system of distinct series
which set up correspondences between each other, in-
tersecting at key points and producing an overall field of
meaning. Except for a selection from the old shop signs,
the photographs gathered together here form part of the
series entitled "Picturesque Paris." From one end to the
other of a series that he worked on throughout his career, Atget used his gift for the "lyrical understanding of
the street"[4] to photograph the Parisians about their daily
activities. Beneath Atget's lens, the small trades or *petits
métiers* traditionally associated with the representation
of urban life became metonymic figures of the city: for
him, they *were* the city. The series is prolonged by the old
shops, the sales displays, and the vitrines, which place a
stronger accent on the effects that the new commercial
developments had exerted on the city.

The Petits Métiers and Urban Theater

The motif of the *petit métier* is inscribed in a long iconographic tradition stretching back to the sixteenth century.
In Atget's work, the representation of these wandering
tradesmen in the period 1899-1901 is characterized by the
relation they entertain with their immediate environment:
the street. Atget chose to photograph a series of *petit métiers*
on Saint-Médard square. The square is represented as the
stage of an urban theater on which the actors of everyday
life present themselves in their characteristic roles, or en-
ter situations of interplay between each other. Following
a logic developed throughout his work, Atget engages in
the representation of a specific urban context which is

constituted against the backdrop of another city, that of Baron Haussmann, the city prefect charged with the modernization of Paris. Outside Saint-Médard square or other physiognomies recalling Old Paris, the *petits métiers* are isolated figures around whom Haussmann's city appears as a fuzzily uniform background.

In this entire series, Atget adopts a procedure based on gradual specification. He begins with a dense, busy crowd, to arrive progressively at a frontal, individual representation of the wandering merchants.

Atget, the Theater and the City

As his biography and many aspects of his photographic production make evident, Atget was above all a theater actor suddenly converted to photography.[5] In 1879, at the age of twenty-two, he entered the Conservatory under the direction of Edmond Got, an actor at the Comédie Française. But his military service rapidly came to interfere with the completion of his studies, and in 1881 he was definitively expelled from the course. He then became a wandering actor until 1888, the approximate date of his conversion to photography. Although Atget ceased to be a professional actor at this time, he maintained his interest in the theater and continued to study it, as numerous books which accompanied him throughout his lifetime can testify.[6] He referred to himself as a "dramatic artist" until 1912, at which date he took up the designation of "author-publisher of a photographic anthology of Old Paris." Finally, from 1904 to 1913 he gave lectures on the theater in the Popular Universities, at the House of the People, the Socialist Cooperative, and the School of Advanced Studies in the Social Sciences. Atget retained a pronounced taste for the theater, translated in his photography by constant analogies between the two practices. His theatrical career was therefore short in the strict sense, but extended in various other forms.

In the "Picturesque Paris" series, and more broadly, throughout his entire oeuvre, Atget used photography to describe the different aspects of a city opposed in many respects to the forms taken on by the spectacular, hygienist modernization of Haussmann and his successors. Precipitated by the 1848 revolution, Haussmann's building campaigns forcefully completed the transformation of Paris that had begun during the Restoration. The aim of the reigning power was to build a modern city that would meet the new demands of industrialization, a major one being the smooth and efficient circulation of men and merchandise. The great boulevards opened up the necessary traffic routes, while at the same time permitting the dedensification of the old center of Paris and of the insalubrious *quartiers,* such as the Bastille, where revolutionary pockets had traditionally subsisted. Haussmann's administration destroyed a great deal, but also edified symbols. Thus the monuments raised by the city from 1853 onward partake of an overall project that aimed to inscribe the traces of a political power in the urban landscape. In the preface to his *Histoire de la France urbaine,* Georges Duby stresses the political stakes of such a project: "The city is the great theater of civic pride. This stage demanded a decor. So that the parades of power could unfold in a seeming way, urban space had to be shaped in a certain fashion. It had to be governed, compelled to regularity by the strict disposition of what is quite rightly termed urbanism."[7] Hence the grand perspectives that focus the gaze on monument-symbols or "target-monuments," as opposed to the "signal-monuments" of the middle ages.[8]

The effect of these building campaigns was to unleash the nostalgic vein of the champions of Old Paris, such as Victor Fournel, who expressed his disarray in his book *Paris nouveau et Paris futur:* "I am the plaintive and powerless cry of the retreating Paris, against the Paris to come." Even if the author recognizes that "hygiene is an excellent thing," he hastens to add that "so is art: it would be best to combine them together, rather than to oppose them," for "there are only three places left in Paris where one can find a shadow of its vanished physiognomy: the Montagne Sainte-Geneviève, the Cité and the Marais."[9] Yet many aspects of Atget's art distance it from the nostalgic note that sounds in this lament. Though Atget effectively made the city a personal and political preoccupation, this should not be confused or conflated with the concern to preserve Old Paris. For his work clearly outstrips the often narrow notion of the protection of an historical heritage.[10]

The Public Square as the Stage of an Urban Theater
Remaining on the margins of the various forms of nostalgia, Atget appears to have been far more concerned with the legibility of the old city. Thus when he photographs Saint-Médard square, beyond the representation of the *petits métiers,* he applies himself to the description of the physiognomy of Old Paris as sketched out in the urban tissue, where the popular life of the *quartier* still subsists. Indeed, it was this minor urban tissue that was most often destroyed by the Haussmann administration in order to disencumber space around the monuments. The Viennese architect and art historian Camillo Sitte called the urbanistic process heralded by Haussmann "the modern disease of disencumbering."[11] In his book *The Art*

of Building Cities, published in 1889, Sitte analyzed this movement: "The meaning of disencumbered squares in the city centers (forums or marketplaces) has become essentially different. Only rarely are they now used for the great popular festivals, and everyday life continually retreats further away. Often they fulfill no other function than to procure more air and light, to break the monotony of the sea of houses, or, at most, to free up the perspective on one important edifice or another, so as to better highlight its architectonic effect."[12] As a result of such processes, Gustave Kahn could unequivocally declare in 1901: "The origin of the square is the marketplace."[13]

In Atget's Saint-Médard series, the public square is an urban frame within which the motif of the *petit métier* is extended to scenes of everyday life, that is to say, to the activities indisputably linked to the morphology of a *quartier*. In this series, Atget locates the tradesmen in their immediate environment. That environment is the street, where, as Arlette Farge writes, " the mechanisms of the use and appropriation of space, the links between places and forms of communication, the exchanges that spring up and fade away, can all be singled out and inventoried. It is in the street that a certain ritualization of spatial usage and its inevitable contrary can be perceived."[14] The photographs of the *petits métiers* stage the actors of everyday life in their mutual interrelation. Figures seen in profile mimic buying and selling, conversation or seduction. Spatial practices are established, and, to continue Arlette Farge's description, "these activities also sketch out the aesthetic and emotional uses of the city."[15] To capture the bustling scenes of Saint-Médard square, Atget used a long focal-length lens, which had the effect of creating an immersion of the gaze in the crowd, but also, and more importantly, of juxtaposing – even crushing together – the various picture planes (foreground, middleground, background, etc.). Finally, following a logic close to that of documentary, Atget proceeded by successive phases. Starting from the crowd, he worked toward the individuation of the tradesman, using a process which confers a progressively greater intimacy on the space.

Theatrical Figures

Atget marked off the decor of his urban theater with Saint-Médard square, taken as the model of an environment where human and social activities intertwine. But as the individuation of the tradesman grows increasingly precise, the city, in its presence as an artifact, is dissolved by the double effect of blurring and of light. Through this process, perfectly mastered by Atget, the figure of the *petit métier* steps free of Haussmann's city, which is no longer his. Only the *Lampshade peddler* contradicts this system: the architectonic elements of this image are structural and share in the overall dynamics of the image. This status as an exception lends the image a special quality, making it the icon of all the *petits métiers*.

Some of Atget's *petits métiers* are related to what may be called standing portraits. In this form, the wandering merchants are transmuted into emblematic figures of the city and its urban theater, as the photographer conceived them. In the series of standing portraits, it is no longer the mimetic dimension of the *petit métier* that is stressed – a dimension found in the Saint-Médard photographs – but rather an imaginary register which is conveyed by the figure. Frontal by nature, these standing portraits deny the exotic effect of a "snapshot" taken without the knowledge of those concerned. The tradesmen "pose" at a standstill

Saint-Médard. 1898

before the lens, loaded down with their wares which become the attributes and distinctive signs of a mobile activity. Consubstantial to the tradesman's body, the wares in all their forms metamorphose, and the excrescences of this mutation are added like new, supplementary extremities, in an organic flourish which is close to ornamentation. On some of Atget's photographs the arms disappear beneath the exuberant forms. A serpentine line of wicker baskets winds around a vendor's body, ending in a kind of protuberance. On the hypertrophied body of the *Wire basket peddler,* the burst of light reveals a very fine, transparent membrane constituted by the merchandise. Elsewhere, the round forms of the lampshades "geometricize" a part of the peddler's body, while lighter forms on the other side provide him with an organic growth.[16] These "assemblages"[17] can be compared with the *Manager's Costume* created seventeen years later by Picasso for the decor of the play *Parade.* In this costume, the actor bears the objects of his commerce – buildings – like the wandering tradesmen carry their wares of the day. In the program of the play, Guillaume Apollinaire qualified Picasso's costumes as "fantastic constructions" and spoke, for the first time, of "sur-realism."[18]

As a man of the theater, Atget was greatly interested in costumes and particularly in their representation through engraving. He executed photographic reproductions of engravings by Abraham Bosse and Daumier in the *Recueil de Caignières* anthology. In these reproductions, certain standing portraits show poses similar to those of the *petits métiers.* But the analogy with the theater continues elsewhere: the tradesmen posing for the camera are like actors "pointing themselves out" on the stage of the urban theater. In the language of the French theater, the

Flower seller, 1898-1900

pointe was the climactic moment in the play when the actor stood forth alone in the middle of the stage to deliver his monologue facing the public.[19] This convention had the particularity of interrupting the action unfolding on the stage, just as the tradesmen cease their activity for the time in which they consciously engage in a process of representation.

The Mobility of the Tradesman

Urban mobility is imposed on the tradesman, for whom it is a necessity. He who is excluded from the commercial privilege of fixity is obliged to adopt ambulatory strategies, bringing all his wares with him and aspiring to maximum visibility, in quest of higher earnings.

In the second half of the nineteenth century, when the daily volume of garbage grew considerably with the progress of industry and consumption, the activity of the tradesmen changed and became linked to a growing industry of refuse. The ragpicker then appeared, as part of the "lumpen proletariat" – that final fall from the scale of social class hierarchies which posed, in Walter Benjamin's words, "the mute question as to where the limit of human misery lay."[20] The figure of the ragpicker quickly came to function in the social imaginary as the symbol of the entire population of small tradesmen, with their urban mobility. But this real mobility only existed in the circuits sketched out by the successive stages of the "recycling" of refuse. Once gathered up and hauled by the ragpickers to the limits of the city, the refuse was transformed, before acquiring the new surplus value which would be realized through sale in the centripetal city. It was the wandering peddlers who, as the complements of the ragpickers, assured the return of these new objects

to the place where they had been cast aside but little before. At antipodes from the objective gaze that analyzes
this figure as "the limit of human misery," many pre-
ferred to take the ragpicker as an allegory of the
regeneration of the social body by means of its refuse.
Jules Janin considered the ragpicker's basket as "a great
catch-basin into which flows all the scum of the social
body."[21] Baudelaire had already used the figure of the
ragpicker as part of his larger metaphor of the poet as a
hero of modernity:

"Here is a man charged with picking up the debris of a
day in the capital. Everything that the great city has cast
off, everything it has lost, everything it has disdained, everything it has broken, is catalogued and collected by him.
He consults the archives of debauchery, the treasuries of
trash. He makes a selection, an intelligent choice; like a
miser with his gleaming hoard, he gathers the scraps of
refuse which, chewed over by divine Industry, will become objects of utility or pleasure."[22]

In the series of Atget's *petits métiers,* the evocation of this
mobility reaches its culmination in the figure of the
Ragpicker hauling his imposing load. The standing por-
trait of the ragpicker in the street – for here the personage
cannot be separated from the merchandise he transports
– makes him a monumental figure of the city. Following
the model of the other photographs in the series, the ar-
chitectural elements seem to disintegrate around him,
setting up a disjunction between that which is stable –
the architectonic – and the mobile character of the ragpicker. Moreover, the pose that he strikes, the visible
tension of his arms and his advancing leg are elements
that evoke the movement and the urban dynamics of
such a figure.

Ragpicker, Avenue des Gobelins. June 1901

In 1912, this photograph was reused by Atget in an album of sixty prints, which he entitled *Zoniers*. The album describes the inhabitants and the site of the former military zone on the edge of the city, condemned by the administration since 1898. Tellingly, and for the first time since the *petits métiers,* Atget carried out portraits for the series. On one of the album's prints, a ragpicker poses before his hand-drawn cart in a position identical to that of the ragpicker hauling his load in the city, photographed twelve years before. This reprise is the sign of a deliberate correspondence between the two series. The inhabitants of the Zone – most of them ragpickers – pose in their environment which stands out in its slightest details, unlike the blurry city of the tradesmen: here Atget stresses the description of the immediate context. Through this relation between the album *Zoniers* and the series of *petits métiers,* it becomes evident that for the ragpicker the city is often nothing more than a place of transit from which he is forcibly excluded. Writing about this exclusion in his book *Paris capitale du monde,* Texier noted that "every boulevard thrust beyond the fortifications a mass of poor devils whom Paris wanted no more... and for the first time in history one saw this strange, unheard-of, anti-Christian reality: a city that excluded the poor and wished only to be inhabited by the rich."[23]

Paradoxically, the everyday experience of footloose freedom in the city – a condition rare in the nineteenth century and still reserved for the wealthy – was to become a recurrent theme of bohemian literature, through the association of the figure of the ragpicker and that of the Baudelairean *flâneur.*[24] One would have to await the simultaneous rise of department stores and of mass transportation, particularly the metro, for the "democratization" of this

Poterne des Peupliers, Zone dwellers (13th arrondissement). 1913

experience and its revelation in the new phenomena of mass consumption. The same period is also that of the near-disappearance of the wandering tradesmen.

Social Fantasies and Bourgeois Gazes on the Tradesmen

Social Fantasies and Uncertain Taxonomy

The small tradesmen, and particularly the figure of the ragpicker, haunted the social fantasies of the nineteenth century. Like the people in general, they were considered part of the "laboring classes" or the "dangerous classes," and this confusion over their proper identification partook of an apprehension which was rendered all the more complex by the fact that the nineteenth century had effectively known numerous popular uprisings. In a work which was to become famous, Louis Chevalier posed the question of these indecisive frontiers: "For the Parisian bourgeoisie, the laboring classes are on the fringes of the city and must remain there, like those categories of the population which, in earlier epochs, were confounded with the criminal groups."[25] And yet toward the mid-nineteenth century, when their existence was threatened by the new economic era on the horizon, the small tradesmen appeared as something like an image of continuity. This *populace* – a derogatory term in French[26] – could similarly reflect a reassuring image that symbolized the permanence of the Ancien Régime traditions, of the city prior to the urban developments attendant on industrialization: "The spirit of speculation, steam power, the invention of new trades, the growth of fortunes and the pooling of capital allowed for the grouping and ordered disposition of the myriad of ambulatory peddlers who now wait at home for the purchase that they formerly set out to provoke."[27] The slow replacement of the small tradesmen by the great mass of the "industrial proletariat"[28] endowed those once identified as the "laboring classes" with the picturesque charms henceforth to be associated with Old Paris, which, in Victor Fournel's words, was "nothing but an incessant symphony from one end to the other, harmonizing all the provocative notes struck by the voices of the wandering merchants."[29] Indeed, it was after the *petits métiers* had been definitively condemned to disappearance that their identification and classification into types began to be precisely annotated.

From Historical "Object" to Folklore

From the 1850s onwards, the wandering tradesmen became possible "historical objects"[30] and entered the field of the new folklorical current that was fed around the same time by a certain French elite, including Champfleury, the author of the famous manifesto *Du Réalisme*.[31] This constitution as objects of an historiographical discourse becomes apparent in a typology used by numerous authors, such as Victor Fournel in his work *Les Cris de Paris, types et physionomies d'autrefois* (1888). However, the types established in these works are too often related to the genre of caricature, with its prefabricated ideas. Thus, on the visual representations that accompany the texts, the people remain ugly and frightening. Folklore appears in order to "save" a threatened if not already vanished popular culture. Where the tradesmen were concerned, the folklorists sought, if not to preserve them, then at least to evoke their existence in a more-or-less recent past, through narratives and visual representations.[32] Michel de Certeau has distinguished two periods of folklore, which he defines as "an exoticism of the interior."[33] The first period is situated at the close of the eighteenth century and involves, for example, the postrevolutionary "rusticophilia"[34] of Nicolas Restif de la Bretonne, who sought an original purity in the "confusion of traditional hierarchies." The second stage fits into the period 1850-90, when folklore reaches its veritable apogee. In 1857, the folklorical musicologist Kastner published *Les voix de Paris,* a work in which the vendors' cries are placed within the lineage of medieval polyphony. For Kastner, the cries of the small tradesmen are something like the city's acoustic blazon. In a similar vein, Alfred Franklin attempted to reconstruct the lost aspect of Old Paris with the musical color conveyed by the criers, in his works *La Vie privée d'autrefois* and *Les Rues et Cris de Paris au XIIIe siècle.* Over and above their specific qualities, these works guaranteed the tradesmen a "reasoned integration" into what Michel de Certeau calls "the cultural assimilation of a now reassuring museum."[35]

The Experience of the Bourgeois Interior in the Nineteenth Century

The experience of exoticism in the folklore of the street finds its refuge in the reassuring intimacy of the nineteenth-century bourgeois interior. Inaugurated by Nicolas Restif de la Bretonne and Louis Sebastian Mercier, the theme of social marginality found a favorable echo among men of letters. The bohemian milieu, in particular, would constantly identify with the image culled from the margins – and even project itself there – or it would idealize a way of living which would then be quickly reproved, in order to maintain social distinctions.

Adopting the profile of the perfect bohemian, Alexandre Privat d'Anglemont describes the Zone and the Cité Doré as "the land of joy, of dreams, of letting-go, laid down by chance in the heart of a despotic empire."[36] The bourgeoisie needed this marginality to define its own frontiers.[37] And in a highly significant way, Privat d'Anglemont brought his text to a close on this idea: "A simulacrum of property, attaching these misfortunates to the earth, assures them against the wicked thoughts and evil counsel of poverty, while giving the higher classes a security which they cannot have with the agglomeration of indigents, vagabonds, and beggars who gather in the rented rooms of these foul neighborhoods."[38] For Privat the frontiers are clear, and in his writing marginality finally has both a limiting and a constitutive function.

The gaze projected into the streets – in 1858, Victor Fournel entitled one of his books "What One Can See in the Streets of Paris" – produced and nourished what Walter Benjamin called "panoramic literature," in which the highly developed genre of "physiologies," or the examination of types in the street, occupied a predominant place. Instituted by a rash of titles – in the same year as Victor Fournel, Louis Reybaud wrote a novel entitled "What One Can See in a Street" – this gaze sought to encompass social marginality in the aesthetic experience of the fantastic, as seen from the interior of the bourgeois apartment. An album of photographs held at the Bibliothèque Nationale, entitled *Mœurs et types de la Rue: Métiers (1858-1870)* provides a perfect illustration of this fantasy: in one of the photographs, a man gazes on the street through a looking-glass from a photographer's studio, that is to say, from a reconstituted bourgeois interior.

It was Walter Benjamin who most deeply probed the "phantasmagorias of the interior," considering "habitation in its most extreme form as a mode of existence of the nineteenth century."[39] "From this," he wrote, "sprang the phantasmagorias of the interior. This represented the universe for the private citizen. In it he assembled the distant in space and in time. His drawing-room was a box in the world-theater."[40] Thus Victor Fournel writes in his novel that "Madame… believes herself to be quite daring, and her longest voyages are almost always voyages around a living room."[41] For Benjamin, the experience of the street in the nineteenth century most often was only accessible through that of the interior. Similarly, "the street becomes a dwelling for the *flâneur*; he is as much at home among the façades of the houses as a citizen is in his four walls."[42]

Two Modes of Representing the Petit Métier

The first clearly recognizable representations of the *petits métiers* (also known as *cris de Paris*) date from around the sixteenth century. Sketched in the seventeenth century by Pierre Brebriette, Abraham Bosse, and Henri Bonnart, then disseminated through engravings, they had come to constitute an established genre when François Boucher, Edme Bouchardon, Watteau and others took them up and ennobled them in the eighteenth century. Under the impetus of the folklore vogue in the nineteenth century, amplified by the industrial revolution, they formed the object of an extraordinary resurgence of interest, in parallel with the associated literature. This "renaissance" came about after an almost total interruption in the representation of the *petits métiers* during the revolutionary period. A new language to describe the "laboring classes" was elaborated through these representations.[43]

In the first half of the nineteenth century, the representations wavered between two extremes. On one hand were the grotesque images – like mass-produced Epinal prints – of a poverty-stricken population moving through a somber urban decor (*Cris de Paris et mœurs populaires,* drawings by Victor Adam, lithographs by Mercier, 1822). On the other were the images of idealized figures of the people, placed halfway between an urban decor and the pastoral dream of a natural environment already doomed to disappearance (*Costume of Paris,* drawings and engravings by J.J. Challon, London, 1820, and *Les Cris de Paris,* lithographs by Prodhomme, 1848). In the second half of the nineteenth century one can observe the development of engraving toward the genre of the "street types"; most often a comfortable fit emerges between the production of images and of the literature dealing with the same subject. *Etudes contemporaines, types parisiens,* a collection of lithographs by Lemercier in 1850, established the types of the *petits métiers* along the lines of the recent model of taxonomy. Then, from the 1890s onward, a new genre of engraving came to align itself on the effects produced by photography, also used as a means to fix these "street types." The chromolithographs of L. Borgex in 1900, for example, borrow the "snapshot" aspect of photography. In 1904 Jacques Beltrand made wood engravings to illustrate the volume of poetry in prose by Tristan Klingsor, *Petits métiers de Paris.* The engravings were executed on the basis of Atget's *petit métier* series, without any mention of his name. In his preface to the book, Roger Marx describes Beltrand as a "plebeian portraitist" and betrays, though not explicitly, the borrowing from photography: associating Klingsor's prose and Beltrand's illustrations, he evokes "social investigation" and the "fugitive visions

that compose the living museum of the street." He continues: "No type fails to come take its place here, surprised
unawares and defined in the familiarity of its professional
guise." This description is far from Atget's work in many
respects. Yet the the notion of the "social investigation"
brings it surprisingly close to the "social fantastic" of which
Pierre Mac Orlan spoke in the preface of the first posthu-
mous book on the photographer, published in 1930.[44]

In the work of the photographic primitives – the term
primitive being adopted from the history of painting
and used to designate the French calotypists[45] – the *petit métier* is but rarely represented, and is not treated
according to the preponderant model offered by engraving, but derives rather from the field of painting.
For the primitives and even more for their partisans, the
picturesque "motif" of the small tradesmen seems to
hold no other interest than the picturesque effects it produces on the "photographic print."[46] For the new
mechanical process of the calotype – which Francis Wey
prefers to designate by its synonym, "heliography" – per-
mits the transfer of an image onto paper, unlike the
daguerreotype. As Wey writes: "It seems that through the
transition onto paper, the mechanism springs to life; the
camera seems to rise to the level of an intelligence that
combines effects, simplifies execution, interprets nature…
sometimes photography proceeds by masses, disdaining
detail like a skillful master, justifying the theory of sac-
rifices, and lending here the advantage to the form, there
to the opposition of tones."[47] The results obtained present pictorial analogies, which critics and photographers
themselves were quick to point out, in their desire for le-
gitimation. This led Charles Bauchal in 1852 to
distinguish, as in painting, two schools of photographers,

the "colorists" and the "draftsmen"; he saw Charles Nègre, in his *Ramoneurs en marche* (1851), as an "eminently colorist photographer who recalls Rembrandt's drawings."[48] Far from the aesthetic concerns embodied by the primitives were the commercial photo studios of the Second Empire, with their sometimes lucrative production (Disdéri, for instance, built a fortune on his patented visiting cards). They took a quite different approach to the representation of the *petits métiers*. Their production was principally defined by the great mass of portraits which accounted for the bourgeoisie's infatuation with the new art, excoriated by Baudelaire in the *Salon de 1859*. In the normative space of the photo studio which reproduced the intimacy of the bourgeois interior, the intrusion of the small tradesman, and more generally of the working world in any form, produces an incongruous, disjunctive image.[49] Here and there in such photographs we find a mason armed with a trowel, busy about the foot of a fictive brick wall posed on an interior carpet, or, at the same place, a street merchant with a display of fruits and vegetables. Against a backdrop of highly contrived poverty, L. d'Olivier photographs some traveling Italian minstrels – *pifferari* – lying on the floor (1854), Delton photographs a wandering merchant before a picturesque landscape painted on canvas (1862), and Van de Gend, a porter in a studio (1864).[50] Stereoscopic views – "those Epinal images of photographic civilization"[51] – exploit these staged scenes with the spectacular force of the relief obtained through their optical mechanism. But the interior masks the realities of the working world. These procedures lead to an abstraction of the everyday environment and travesty a population by covering over its image with a normative discourse. Often the representations are no more than fabricated scenes where actors take the place of the people in order to play a role far from their own, pushing caricature to its extreme. Such was the opinion of Disdéri, who in his 1862 book *L'art de la photographie* judged stereoscopics to be "a revolting masquerade rendered even more odious by the extreme reality of the relief."[52]

Thus Atget's series of *petits métiers* closes a long iconographic tradition which in the nineteenth century, under the impetus of folklore and with the invention of photography, took on polysemic, fantasmatic forms. There is no folklore in Atget's work, but instead an approach that has more to do both with documentary, for the tradesmen in Saint-Médard square, and with the great tradition of the eighteenth-century engravers, for the emblematic figures of the city. His gaze on the small tradesmen is not a projection from the interior into the street, but an immersion in the crowd culminating in a frontal, individual representation.

Old Shops and Vitrines: Archaism and Modernity in Atget's Work

Resistances and Formal Recurrences of the Petits Métiers

Ten years after he photographed the *petits métiers*, Atget returned to the "Picturesque Paris" series[53] and once again took an interest in the forms of small commerce in the capital city. In his album *Métiers, boutiques et étalages de Paris* (1912), the small tradesmen have disappeared; the kiosks and modern merchandising displays seem to be the metamorphosis of what now appears as an imposed immobility. Governed by a succession of ordinances that span the nineteenth century,[54] the occupation of space on the public thoroughfare is subjected to numerous constraints and must, in the official language of the police prefects, be contained within its "just boundaries."[55]

In the photographs of this album, the kiosks have replaced the wandering peddlers. They present recurrences and persistences of forms encountered previously in the *petits métiers* as recorded by Atget. Inhabited by those who were formerly mobile, the kiosks often become anthropomorphic (as in the *Newspaper kiosk, Bon Marché square*). The wares deployed outside the kiosk are like the laden arms of the wandering peddlers (*Newspaper kiosk, place Saint-Sulpice*). As to the displays, they spill over into the public street, breaking the fixed frames and blurring the frontiers between the space of the shop and the space of the street. The mannequins of the used clothing stores and the often startling arrangements of merchandise in the second-hand shops offer surprising tableaus to the gaze.

Atget's Modernist Archaism

Brought together in an album entitled *Enseignes and vieilles boutiques* (1911), the photographs of the old shop signs contain two different realities. They partake simultaneously of a concern to constitute an archaeological archive for the salvage of Old Paris and of a play of effects combining portraits of the merchants, reflections on the windows, and the reflected image of Atget himself. Atget provides his portraits with a double frame: the door frame recapitulates that of the photograph. Similarly he amuses himself by substituting his own body for that of others through the reflection on the windowpanes, thus obtaining the grotesque silhouette of a dwarfish figure with a large, deformed head (*The Drum*).

When photographing the old Paris shops, Atget evokes a certain physiognomy of commerce described through the façades, which serve a heuristic function. The openings of the façades are deep black gaps whose obscurity cuts into the volume of the building's architecture. These rifts are carefully arranged so as to convey the patterns of circulation characteristic of the shops, which require communication between the commercial areas and the domestic world, between private and public space. Atget perceives this often vernacular architecture, with its add-on principle of construction, as an architecture of contiguous, perfectly intelligible spaces, as in the photograph *Shop on Broca Street.* Here the play of spaces is distinguished by the composition, but also by the framing of the full and empty zones, as well as the "little theatrical event" illustrated by the woman leaning out the window and linking the spaces together. Here the event is produced entirely by the circulation of entries and exits, as in the denouement of a play at the theater. With the exception of the department-store windows, Atget manifestly refuses to photograph the "modern life" of Paris. His position with respect to modernity is that of a critical artist. While the flux of "Parisian living" unfolds on the major boulevards, Atget pays closer attention to an archaizing Paris. His approach stems from his artistic activity and from his political engagement.[56] In short, Atget works against the grain of the ideology and the myth that sees progress as a benefit to humanity, even when it leads to the catastrophe of 1914-1918. Indeed, Atget ceased all photographic activity during the war. There seems to be a certain archaism in Atget's work which could justifiably be called modernist. In his "metaphysical paintings," De Chirico used archaism to confront

Flower seller, June 1901

heterogeneous realities. The strangeness of his disjunctive associations (a factory smokestack and a Greek statue,
for example) won the favor of the surrealists. One of them,
Louis Aragon, in his *Peasant of Paris* (1926), was in search
of a "feeling of strangeness" which he hoped to find in
the "perception of the unusual." The archaic modernity
of the Parisian passages, condemned to destruction, allowed for an ideal form of this experience. For Aragon,
the Parisian passages were the "harborers of several modern myths" because "it is only today when the pick-axe
threatens them that they have effectively become the
sanctuaries of the ephemeral."[57] In the twentieth century
this perspective on modernity became a "technique of
unveiling."[58] In his "Small History of Photography," Walter
Benjamin, one of the great thinkers of the critique of
progress,[59] said of the surrealist photography prefigured
by Atget that it "gives free play to the politically educated
eye."[60] Similarly, for Benjamin, "Atget almost always passed
by the 'great sights and so-called landmarks'; what he did
not pass by was a long row of boot lasts"[61] (*Corner of the
Carmes Market, Maubert Square*, 1910-1911).

"Bachelor Machines"

Photographs of vitrines hold a special place in Atget's work,
to the extent that they constitute the sole documents of
the modern city – a subject which he had studiously
avoided until then. They are also quite special for their
treatment of light, the result of a masterful technique.
Because of their chronology, content, and the treatment
which they receive, certain vitrines, such as *Boulevard de
Strasbourg, corsets* (1912), can be compared to the photographs of the old shops of archaic Paris. The vitrines of
the department stores are different, and in a certain way

more radical in the aesthetic choice they bring into play. But in any case, these images reflect the humor, irony, and sarcasm of a great artist at the end of his life.

The photographs of the vitrines adorning the great department stores – "those monuments to bourgeois civilization"[62] – develop ideas about the commodity and the new practices of mass consumption. Before Atget, Zola had already sought to make the department store "the poem of modern activity."[63] For him it became a "cathedral of modern commerce, solid and ethereal, made for a people of clients."[64] Historically the department-store vitrine appeared at the moment when commodities were presented to the crowds that came to visit the world exhibitions. Thus the iron and glass used for the exhibition buildings (the Crystal Palace, the Gallery of the Machines, the Grand and Petit Palaces) can also be found in the architecture of the department stores – the Bon Marché, for example, constructed in 1869-1879 by the architect Louis-Auguste Boileau and the engineer Gustave Eiffel. The exhibition, that "subject of delirium in the nineteenth century,"[65] had manifestly became one of the signs of the forward march of industrialism.

Far more than a simple display of manufactured products, the department-store vitrine was a space of theatrical staging for the spectacle of the commodity offered to the gaze of the street, and particularly the gaze of the gawking pedestrian, or *badaud*.[66] In the photograph *Store, Avenue des Gobelins* (1925), the highly sexualized mannequins are frozen in place, and yet despite their immobility they manage to evoke the illusion of dizzying motion. Essentially inorganic, these artificial bodies, born of curiosity cabinets and inspired by automatons, seem somehow to breath life into the commodities. This supernatural world comes close

Shop, 93, rue Broca. 1912

to what Karl Marx describes in his chapter "The Fetishism of the Commodity and its Secret." Taking the example of a wooden table as a commodity, he writes: "It not only stands with its feet on the ground, but, in relation to all other commodities, it stands on its head, and evolves out of its wooden brain grotesque ideas, far more wonderful than if it were to begin dancing of its own free will."[67] In Atget's photographs, the commodities seem to defy the laws of gravity; they appear mingled with the urban decor. More precisely, these photographs reveal at once the bizarre optical effects due to reflections in the vitrine and the staging of the desires of the consumer. The image of the consumer is idealized by the mannequin that allows him to project his desires. Dan Graham, who studied this phenomenon for his own artistic work, has described the process: "The vitrine captures, highlights, and manipulates the latent desires of the chance passer-by and confers an overdetermined subjective meaning to the commodities that it presents 'objectively.'"[68] But while the vitrine triggers desire, the glass physically isolates the consumer who contemplates his pale reflection mingled with the spectacle of the commodity.

Interiors and Theatrical Effigies

Where the contiguous spaces of the shops were perceived in their patterns of circulation, those of the vitrine blend together, interlinked in an ambiguity due to the reflections of the "real transparency"[69] of the glass, as revealed by the light. Similarly, the archaizing shops of Old Paris which appear in Atget's photographs as "double-bottomed boxes"[70] or "magic boxes" contrast sharply with the "optical chambers" of the vitrines, which are close in many respects to the catoptric machines exhibited in

the museums of phantasmagorias in vogue in the nineteenth century. The vitrines present certain analogies with
the optical qualities of these machines, which allowed for
"the replacement of one image for another, a man for a
woman, Pierre for Paul."[71] In the photographs, nature, the
mineral world of the city, the passers-by, and the photographer himself are absorbed into the vitrine-optical
chamber, just as other elements were enclosed within the
catoptric machines.

The inside of the vitrine is a parody of a scenographic
space, just as a scale model can be a parody of architecture. From the outside, the vitrine can offer the framed
viewpoint of a "scenographic cube."[72] As early as 1901
Gustave Kahn regarded the department-store vitrines as
"one or more rectangular boxes of which one of the walls
has been taken away and replaced with glass."[73] To pur-
sue the theatrical metaphor, one can add that this
scenographic reconstruction offers something like the re-
duction of a stage-set from naturalist theater, such as
Antoine's Free Theater in France or Stanislavsky's Theater
of Art in Russia. By its transparency, the glass of the vitrines realizes the stage director's fantasy: to feign the
existence of a "fourth wall." Often in their plays the cur-
tain opened on a reconstituted living room which denied
any opening to the theater. Concerning this refusal of a
theater directly involving the public, Vsevolod Meyerhold
writes: "This theater tirelessly sought the fourth wall, and
that led it to an entire series of absurdities… in this way
it transformed itself into a shop full of museum pieces."[74]
The closed space of the vitrine also reproduces the interior of the bourgeois apartment. In the photographs of
Bon Marché, the mannequins are seated on a comfortable
canapé, posed amidst precious accessories destined for

the ornamentation of a private space. I have evoked the
"phantasmagoria of the interior" described by Benjamin;
in 1910, Atget constituted an album of sixty photographs
which he entitled *Intérieurs parisiens, début du XXᵉ siècle,
pittoresques et bourgeois*. Emptied of their occupants, these
interiors stressed class differences and gave a hint of the
photographer's method and his political convictions.[75]
They are the intimate "portraits" of inhabitants whom
Atget never photographed. Can the enigma that surrounds
this emptiness not be deciphered precisely with the help
of the vitrines photographed fifteen years before, in which
the mannequins are but the effigies of those in whom
Benjamin discerned "a tendency to compensate for the
absence of any trace of private life in the big city"?[76]

The act of photographing a city had a particular meaning for Atget, and it had to meet the political standards
he had set himself throughout his life. His refusal to photograph Haussmann's Paris went hand in hand with his
concern to render visible its outcasts. In his entire body
of work, the right to the city was enjoyed only by the
wandering tradesmen, the vagabonds, the inhabitants
of the Zone, and the prostitutes. Indeed, it is this continuity and this coherency among all the differences that
confers on Atget's photographs such a unique power of
evocation.

Notes

1. See Jean-François Chevrier, "La carte et la boussole," preface to "Colloque Atget" (proceedings of the colloquium, Collège de France, June 14-15, 1985), in *Photographies*, special issue, 1986, p. 7.

2. Peter Gallasi, "Faire dialoguer Kertész avec Picasso et Matisse," *Le Monde*, March 26, 1996.

3. See Rosalind Krauss, *Le photographique: Pour une théorie des écarts*, Macula, Paris, 1990, pp. 48-53.

4. Walker Evans, "The Reappearance of Photography," *Hound and Horn*, October-December 1931, pp. 125-128.

5. For an outline of the photographer's biography, see the study by Maria Morris Hambourg, "A biography of Eugène Atget," in *The Work of Atget, Volume II: The Art of Old Paris*, New York, The Museum of Modern Art, 1982. Also see Jean Leroy, *Atget, magicien du Vieux Paris en son époque*, Paris, Pierre Balbo, 1975, reissued, Paris, Paris Audiovisuel/Pierre Jean Balbo, 1992.

6. Drawing on her examination of a photograph of his interior, Maria Morris Hambourg has listed the titles of the works visible on his shelves; they include *Les anciens théâtres de Paris* by Georges Cain, a study on *Le théâtre de la Révolution*, and *Notre époque au théâtre* by Alfred Capus. There are also complete editions of Eschylus, Sophocles, Euripides, and works by Racine, Corneille, Molière, Voltaire, Casimir Delavigne, Shakespeare, Lord Byron, Victor Hugo, Alexandre Dumas *père*, Alexandre Dumas *fils*, Alfred de Musset, Alfred de Vigny, and Emile Augier. See Maria Morris Hambourg, op. cit., p. 21.

7. Georges Duby, preface to *Histoire de la France urbaine*, Paris, Seuil, 1980-1985.

8. François Loyer, *Paris XIXᵉ siècle: l'immeuble et la rue*, Paris, Hazan, 1987, p. 287.

9. Victor Fournel, *Paris nouveau et Paris Futur*, Paris, Librairie J. Lecoffre, 1868, p. 3 and pp. 16-18.

10. Atget never directly collaborated with the official "Commission

Municipale du Vieux Paris," despite his personal contacts with Edouard Detaille and Victorien Sardou, both of whom were members of the Commission.

11. See Camillo Sitte, *L'Art de bâtir les villes, l'urbanisme selon ses fondements artistiques*, trans. D. Wieczorek, Paris, Livre et communication, 1990.

12. *Ibid*, p. 4.

13. Gustave Kahn, *L'esthétique de la rue*, Paris, Bibliothèque Charpentier, 1901, p. 149.

14. Arlette Farge, *Vivre dans la rue à Paris au XVIIIᵉ siècle*, Paris, Gallimard/Juliard, 1979, reissued in 1992, p. 9.

15. *Ibid*, p. 11.

16. Arlette Farge speaks of assemblages of objects and bodies, of "body commodities" which extend to join the objects that they bear "in the greatest significance"; see "Le bazar de la rue" (a review of Massin's book *Les Cris de la Ville, commerces ambulants et petits métiers de la rue*, Paris, Gallimard, 1978), in *Vrbi* 1, September 1979, pp. XCVII-XCVIII.

17. *Ibid*.

18. Apollinaire's program text is entitled "Parade et l'Esprit Nouveau" (1917); reprinted in Guillaume Apollinaire, *Chroniques d'art, 1902-1918*, edited with preface and notes by l. -C. Breunig, Paris, Gallimard, 1960, pp. 532-534.

19. See Richard Sennet, *The Fall of Public Man*, New York, Norton, 1992.

20. Walter Benjamin, *Charles Baudelaire: A Lyric Poet in the Era of High Capitalism*, London, NLB, 1973, trans. Harry Zohn, p. 19 (chapter "The *Bohème*").

21. Jules Janin, "Les petits métiers," in *Le livre des cent-et-un*, vol. III, Paris, Ladvocat, 1831, p. 342.

22. Charles Baudelaire, *Les paradis artificiels*, Paris, Gallimard, Le Livre de poche, 1964, p. 74.

23. Edmond Auguste Texier and Albert Kaempen, *Paris capitale du monde*, Paris, Hetzel, 1867, p. 3.

24. See Walter Benjamin, *Charles Baudelaire: A Lyric Poet in the Era of High Capitalism*, op. cit.

25. Louis Chevalier, *Classes laborieuses et classes dangereuses à Paris pendant la première moitié du XIXe siècle*, Paris, Plon, 1958, pp. 449-454.

26. "The populace? Such indeed is the term most commonly employed to designate those popular and criminal groups, mixed up in the same indiscriminately political and criminal enterprises, a term which takes its place in our bourgeois vocabulary alongside the words 'barbarous,' 'wild,' 'nomadic.'" Louis Chevalier, op. cit., p. 454.

27. Victor Fournel, *Les cris de Paris, types et physionomies d'autrefois*, Paris, Librairie de Firmin-Didot, 1888, pp. 70-71.

28. In his work, op. cit., p. 454, Louis Chevalier quotes Daniel Stern, who evokes "the excessive growth of an important fraction of the popular classes which, as though destined by a combination of circumstances, came to form a class apart, like a nation within the nation, which began to be designated by a new word: the industrial proletariat."

29. Victor Fournel, op. cit., p. 5.

30. Michel de Certeau notes that folklore will henceforth constitute the people "as an object of *science*"; see Michel de Certeau, "La beauté du mort" (written in collaboration with Dominique Julia and Jacques Revel), in *La culture au pluriel*, Paris, Christian Bourgois, 1993, p. 51.

31. On the illusory idea of a childlike people reflected without deformations and appearing before our eyes in perfect purity, see Champfleury, *Histoire de l'imagerie populaire*, Paris, E. Dentu, 1869, reissued, Bayac, Roc de Bourzac, 1992. Champfleury writes: "These plates are the mirrors of childhood days whose reflection is unalterable. An entire past unfolds before these old images contemporaneous with our childhood... Their eyes, at least, were not corrupted by the effrontery of modern *chic*" (pp. XXXV-

XXXVI). Also see the letter by Champfleury to George Sand in 1853, reprinted in Champfleury, *Du Réalisme, Correspondance*, Paris, Éditions des Cendres, 1991, pp. 23-24.

32. For a complete study of the representations of the *petits métiers* from the sixteenth to the eighteenth centuries and of the related literature see the work by Vincent Milliot, *Les Cris de Paris ou le peuple travesti, les représentations des petits métiers (XVIᵉ - XVIIIᵉ siècles)*, Paris, Publications de la Sorbonne, 1995.

33. Michel de Certeau, "La beauté du mort," op. cit., pp. 45-72, p. 48 for the quote.

34. *Ibid*, p. 48.

35. See Michel de Certeau, op. cit, p. 53: "Yet the folklorist's curiosity is not exempt from tacit intentions: he wishes to situate, connect, assure. His interest is like the inverse of censorship: a reasoned integration. Thus popular culture is defined as a heritage... Genealogy and comparativism therefore come to reinforce the existence of a unit in the French repertory, in which a *French mentality* is expressed. Thus anchored, the popular domain ceases to be a disquieting world... Folklore guarantees the cultural assimilation of a now reassuring museum."

36. Alexandre Privat d'Anglemont, *Paris Anecdote* (1854), Paris, Les Éditions de Paris, 1984, p. 174.

37. See the article by Dietmar Rieger, "Ce qu'on voit dans les rues de Paris: marginalités sociales et regards bourgeois," *Romantisme* 59, 1988, pp. 20-29.

38. Privat d'Anglemont, op. cit., pp. 182-183.

39. Walter Benjamin, "L'intérieur, la trace," *Paris, capitale du XIXᵉ siècle, le Livre des passages*, trans. Jean Lacoste, Paris, Cerf, 1993, p. 239.

40. Walter Benjamin, "Exposé de 1939," *Paris, capitale du XIXᵉ siècle, le Livre des passages*, op. cit., p. 52.

41. Victor Fournel, op. cit., p. 2.

42. Walter Benjamin, *Charles Baudelaire: A Lyric Poet in the Era of High Capitalism*, op. cit., p. 37 (chapter "The *Flâneur*").

43. See the chapter "Les impasses de la source-reflet," in Vincent Milliot, op. cit., p. 47: "One finds, among certain folklorists... a will to rediscover the characteristics of a national identity through the history of cultural productions. The cries of Paris, situated in an implicit hierarchy of aesthetic and social values, additionally offer an opening to the constitutive characteristics of popular identity, by virtue of the same approach. This first reading of the cries as expressing the timeless soul of the people is completed by a second reading, which derives from the realist aesthetic as embodied by Champfleury, for example."

44. Pierre Mac Orlan (preface), *Atget photographe de Paris*, Paris, Henri Jonquières, 1930, pp. 12-13.

45. See André Jammes and Eugénia Parry Janis, *The Art of french calotype (with a critical dictionary of photographers, 1845-1870)*, Princeton, Princeton University Press, 1983.

46. On the importance of the print as a material and artistic reality, see Gustave Le Gray, *Photographie: Traité nouveau théorique et pratique des procédés et manipulations sur papier-sec, humide et sur verre au collodion, à l'albumine*, Lerebours et Secrétan, n.d. [1852], partially reprinted in André Rouillé, *La photographie en France, textes et controverses: une anthologie (1816-1871)*, Paris, Macula, 1989, pp. 98-103: "From my viewpoint, the artistic beauty of a photographic practice always consists, on the contrary, in the sacrifice of certain details, so as to produce an effect which sometimes attains the sublime of art."

47. Francis Wey, "De l'influence de l'héliographie sur les Beaux-Arts," *La Lumière* 1, February 9, 1851, pp. 2-3, reprinted in Rouillé, op. cit., pp. 108-114.

48. Charles Bauchal, "Soirée photographique," *La Lumière* 23, May 29, 1852.

49. André Rouillé, "Les images photographiques du travail sous le Second Empire," *Le Sa See See, Actes de la recherche en sciences sociales* 54, September 1984, pp. 31-43.

50. These two photographs are brought together in *Album mœurs et types de métiers (1858-1870)*, held at the Cabinet des Estampes of the Bibliothèque nationale.

51. Yvan Christ, *La vie familière sous le Second Empire*, Paris, Berger-Levrault, 1977, p. 17.

52. André-Adolphe-Eugène Disdéri, *L'art de la photographie*, introduction by Lafon de Carmasac, Paris, published by the author, 1862, p. 302.

53. I follow the nomenclature of Maria Morris Hambourg, op. cit.

54. See, for example, the ministerial decrees classified under the number F. 18/551 in the Archives nationales.

55. G. Delavau, Prefect of the Police, *Ordonnance concernant les étalages sur la voie publique*, Paris, August 21, 1822.

56. Atget gave classes in the popular universities and assiduously read the left-leaning, antimilitarist, and Dreyfusard newspapers, *L'Avant-garde, La Guerre sociale, La Bataille syndicaliste,* which he donated to the Bibliothèque nationale and the Bibliothèque historique de la ville de Paris.

57. Louis Aragon, *Le Paysan de Paris*, Gallimard, 1926, renewed in 1953, Paris, 1993, pp. 9-21.

58. Jacques Leenhardt, "L'Énigme de l'objet, propos sur la 'métaphysique' chez Giorgio De Chirico et la 'mythologie' chez Aragon," *L'Objet au défi*, anthology by Jacqueline Chénieux-Gendron and Marie-Claire Dumas, C.N.R.S, Ivry-sur-Seine, P.U.F, "Champs des activités surréalistes," 1987, pp. 9-21.

59. See Walter Benjamin, *Sur le concept d'histoire* (1940), in *Écrits français*, ed. Jean-Maurice Monnoyer, Paris, Gallimard, 1991, pp. 343-344, and Michaël Löwy, "Walter Benjamin critique du progrès: à la recherche de l'expérience perdue," *Walter Benjamin et Paris, Colloque international 27-29 juin 1983*, ed. Heinz Wismann, Paris, Cerf, 1986, pp. 629-641.

60. Walter Benjamin, "A Small History of Photography" (1931), *One Way Street and Other Writings,* trans. E. Jephcott, K. Shorter, London, Verso, 1985, p. 251

61. Ibid, p. 250.

62. Michael B. Miller, *Au Bon Marché, 1869-1920, le consommateur apprivoisé*, Paris, Armand Colin, 1987, p. 7 and *passim*.

63. Emile Zola, *Notes pour Au Bonheur des Dames*, Bibliothèque nationale, N.A.F 10277, p. 2.

64. Emile Zola, *Au Bonheur des Dames* (1883), Paris, Le Livre de Poche, 1984, p. 260.

65. Gustave Flaubert, *Dictionnaire des idées reçues*. Also see Philippe Hamon, *Expositions, littérature et architecture au XIXᵉ siècle*, Mayenne, José Corti, 1989.

66. "Yet let us not confuse the *flâneur* with the *badaud*... Beneath the influence of the spectacle, the *badaud* becomes an impersonal being, he is no longer a man: he is the public, he is the crowd." Victor Fournel, *Ce qu'on voit dans les rues de Paris*, Paris, 1858, p. 263.

67. Karl Marx, *Capital*, vol. I, trans. Ben Fowkes, London, New Left Review, 1976, p. 163-64.

68. Dan Graham, "Verre utilisé dans les vitrines, articles dans les vitrines," *Ma position, Écrits sur mes oeuvres*, Villeurbanne, Les Presses du réel, 1992, p. 141; originally published as "Glass Used in Shop Windows/Commodities in Shop Windows," in *Video-Architecture-Television,* Halifax, Nova Sotia College of Art and Design and New York, New York University Press, 1979.

69. See Colin Rowe and Robert Slutzky, *Transparency*, Birkhauser, 1997.

70. In his novel *Cœur d'Acier,* Paul Féval depicts a workshop in Old Paris around the 1850s: "This remarkable establishment began to arouse curiosity... There were people who now began to look on Paris as an immense double-bottomed box, who thought that beneath any paving stone they should find a surprise." Paris, Robert Laffont, 1987, p. 562.

71. Jurgis Baltrusaitis, *Le miroir*, Paris, Aline Almayan/Seuil, 1978, p. 34 and *passim;* also see Max Milner, *La fantasmagorie*, Paris, P.U.F, 1982.

72. Pierre Francastel, "Destruction d'un espace plastique," in *Études de sociologie de l'art*, Éditions Denoël, 1970, p. 224 et *passim*. On the framed view offered by the vitrine, Dan Graham writes: "The vitrine as a frame, or as an optical mechanism, reproduces the form of Renaissance painting's illusory three-dimensional space." *Ma position, Écrits sur mes oeuvres*, op. cit., p. 139.

73. Kahn, Gustave, op. cit., p. 209.

74. Vsevolod Meyerhold, *Écrits sur le théâtre*, vol. I, 1891-1917, Lausanne, La Cité/L'Age d'homme, 1973, p. 102.

75. See Molly Nesbit and Françoise Reynaud, *Intérieurs parisiens, Eugène Atget*, Paris, Carré/Paris-Musées, 1992.

76. "[They attempt] to find that compensation between the four walls of [their] apartment." Walter Benjamin, "Paris, capitale du XIXè siècle, exposé de 1939," op. cit., p. 53. Benjamin makes a telling comment on Atget's photos in his "Small History of Photography," op. cit., p. 251: "The city in these pictures looks cleared out, like a lodging that has not yet found a new tenant."

All titles which Atget gave to his photographs are in italics; any additions or commentaries on the part of the editor are printed in Roman characters.

Petits Métiers

Place Saint-Médard, morning. 1898

Small Market on Place Saint-Médard. 1898

Place Saint-Médard. Flower sellers, 1898

Wandering peddler, Place Saint-Médard, 1898-1899

Place Saint-Médard, September 1899

Place Saint-Médard, September 1899

Edgar Quinet Market. July 1899

Avenue des Gobelins. 1898-1900

Artichoke vendor, Place Saint-Médard, August 1899

Umbrella peddler, Place Saint-Médard, 1898-1899

Baker, September 1899

Mailman. 1899

Newspaper vendor. August 1900

Place Saint-Médard, 5th Arrondissement. Herb vendors, 1899

Cast peddler, Avenue de l'Observatoire, circa 1900

Square keeper, 1898-1900

Lottery, 1898-1900

Place Saint-Médard. 1898

Flower vendors, Place de la Bastille. 1898

Fruit and vegetable vendors, omnibus Châtelet-Villejuif, 1898-1900

Sweeper, 1898-1900

Sweeper, 1898-1900

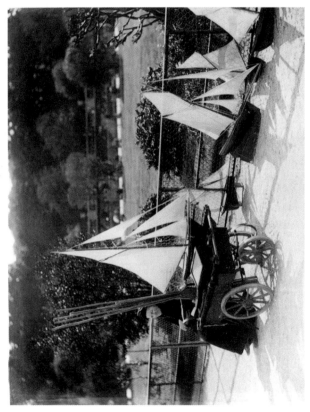

Boat vendor. Luxembourg. 1898

Sharpener. 1898-1899

Carders on the quais, 1898-1900

Carders on the quais, 1898-1900

Boulevard de Clichy, 1898-1900

Flower sellers, 1898-1901

Two vendors on the quais, 1898-1900

Carders on the quais, 1898-1900

Ice-cream vendor, 1898-1900

Beverage seller on the street, 1898–1900

Saint-Germain-des-Prés. Rue de l'Abbaye. Bill posters, 1898

Movers, 1898-1900

Asphalt layers. 1898-1900

Asphalt layers. 1898-1900

Wooden pavement layers. 1898

Pavement layers. 1899-1900

Pavement layers. 1899-1900

Sharpener, September 1899

Fruit and vegetable vendors, 1898-1900

Organ player, 1898-1899

Baker's helper. 1898-1900

Bread vendor. 1899-1900

Sharpener. July 1900

Porcelain mender, 1899

Porter, September 1898

Window washer, June 1901

Quartier Mouffetard, 5th arrondissement. Ragpicker, August 1899

Fort des Halles, 1898-1900

Guitar player. 1899-1900

Small tradesman. Herb vendor, Place Saint-Médard, 1898-1899

Jardin des plantes. Place Vallubert. 1899

Lampshade peddler. Rue Lepic, 1899-1900

Wire basket peddler. 1899-1900

Basket peddler. October 1899

Old Shops and Signs

Newspaper kiosk, Bon Marché square. 1910-1911

Newspaper kiosk, place Saint-Sulpice. 1910-1911

Small key vendor, quai de la Rapée. 1910-1911

Small flower shop, place de la Bastille. 1910-1911

Newspaper vendor, 1898-1900

Ice-cream vendor, Bon Marché square. 1910-1911

Boulevard Saint-Michel. Kiosk, 1898

Shoemaker's shop, corner of rue Garancière, 6th arrondissement

Butcher. Les halles. 1898-1901

The Port-Salut, rue des Fossés Saint-Jaques. 1903

Rue Mouffetard. Milk-coffee vendor, 1898-1901

Small fry shop, rue Mouffetard. 1910-1911

Vegetable shop, rue Mouffetard. 1910-1911

Vegetable shop, 25, rue Charlemagne. 1910-1911

Secondhand dealer, 53, rue Grenéta, 2d arrondissement. 1914

Little grocery, 22, rue Tournefort, 5th arrondissement. 1912

Old shop, 10, rue des Lyonnais, 5th arrondissement. 1914

Shop, 12, rue des Lyonnais, 5th arrondissement. 1914

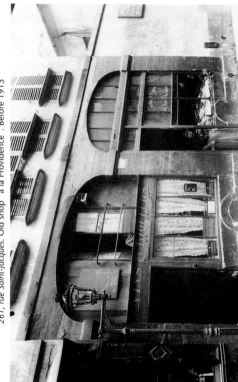

261, rue Saint-Jacques. Old shop "à la Providence". Before 1915

Old shop, 10, rue Donat, 5th arrondissement. 1914

5, rue de la Reynie, 4th arrondissement. Before 1915

Old house. 93, rue Broca. Ca. 1912

The Frank Drinker, rue Norvins, rue Saint-Rustique

Place Dauphine, no. 10. Before 1915

Rue de Clery and Saint-Aboukir

1, rue de Furstenberg. Ancient pillar of the Abbey of Saint-Germain-des-prés

Cabaret, 38, quai de Béthune. 1903

Rue Saint-Germain-l'Auxerrois

Corner of rue de l'Abbaye and rue Bonaparte

Corner of Place Saint-André-des-Arts and rue Hautefeuille, before 1915

Hôtel de Tabellion, 31, rue de Seine

8, rue du Parc Royal

Rue Guénégaud, 6th arrondissement

Old houses, 30 and 32 rue Serpentine. Before 1915

64, rue Saint-Anne, 2nd arrondissement

Balcony, 15, rue du Petit-Pont, 5th arrondissement. 1913

The Hardy Cock. June 1925

The Griffon, 39, quai de l'Horloge. 1903

Shop, Empire style, 21, rue du Faubourg Saint-Honoré. 1902

The Jean Bart, 38, Avenue La Motte-Piquet. 1911

The Armed Man, 25, rue des Blancs-Manteaux. 1901

The he Doe, rue Geoffroy Saint-Hilaire. 1905

The Little Bacchus, rue Saint-Louis-en-l'Ile, 61. 1903

The Drum. 1908

The Little Dunkerque, 3, quai Conti. 1901

The Alarm Clock, 136, rue Amelot. 1903

The Babe Jesus, rue des Bourdonnais, 33. 1901

Cabaret au Beaujolais, 24, rue des Messageries, 10th arrondissement

Cabaret rue Saint-André-des-Arts, 54 (disappeared in 1911). 1900

Cabaret de l'ami Jean, 8, rue Thouin. 1908

Shop of household articles, 340, rue de Vaugirard. 1910-1911

Costume maker, 2, rue de la Corderie. 1910-1911

Secondhand dealer, 32, rue Broca. 1912

Secondhand dealer, boulevard Edgar Quinet. 1910-1911

Men's shop, 16, rue Dupetit-Thouars (Temple district). 1910-1911

Secondhand dealer, 10, avenue Lowendal. 1910-1911

Shop, Halles market. June 1925

Secondhand dealer, 42, rue du Cherche-Midi, 6th arrondissement. 1912

Costume maker, 2, rue de la Corderie. 1910-1911

Shop, Halles market. June 1925

Secondhand dealer, rue des Anglais. 1910-1911

Corner of Carmes Market, Place Maubert. 1910-1911

Rue Mouffetard. 1926

Rue Mouffetard. 1926

Clothing shop and Père Lunette cabaret, rue des Anglais. 1910-1911

Old house, 27, rue des Grands Augustins. 1914

Balcony, 17, rue du Petit-Pont, 5th arrondissement. 1913

A corner of the rue des Lombards, no. 56, 1st arrondissement. 1912

Toy store, 63, rue de Sèvres. 1910-1911

Boulevard de Strasbourg, corsets. 1912

Avenue des Gobelins. 1926-1927

Avenue des Gobelins. 1926

Avenue des Gobelins. 1927

Avenue des Gobelins. 1926-1927

Vitrines

Hairdresser, boulevard de Strasbourg. 1912

Hairdresser, avenue de l'Observatoire. 1926

Hairdresser, Palais Royal. 1926-1927

Toupee store, Palais Royal, 1926-1927

Shop in Les Halles. 1925

Shop in Les Halles. 1925

Store, avenue des Gobelins. 1925

Store, avenue des Gobelins. 1925

Store, avenue des Gobelins. 1925

Store, avenue des Gobelins. 1925

Bon Marché Department Store. 1926-1927

Bon Marché Department Store. 1926-1927

Rue de l'Ecole de Médecine. 1926-1927

Taxidermist, rue de l'Ecole de Médecine. 1926-1927

POCKET ⌗ ARCHIVES
HAZAN

1 - *Alfred Hitchcock,*
   by Serge Kaganski

2 - *Fernando Pessoa,*
   by Maria José de Lancastre
   et Antonio Tabucchi

3 - *The Spanish Civil War,*
   by Abel Paz

4 - *New York in the 1930s,*
   by Samuel Fuller

5 - *Heartfield versus Hitler,*
   by John Willett

6 - *Architecture and Utopia,*
   by Franco Borsi

7 - *Le Havre-New York,*
   by Christian Clères

8 - *Erik Satie,*
   by Ornella Volta

9 - *The French Resistance, 1940-1944*
   by Raymond Aubrac

10 - Atget, *Life in Paris*
   Guillaume Le Gall

11 - *Sports Heroes*
   Michel Butel

12 - *Venetian Palaces*
   Raffaella Russo